How Life Science Works

HOW DO DOLPHINS COMMUNICATE?

LORI MACDHUI

PowerKiDS press.
New York

Published in 2018 by The Rosen Publishing Group, Inc.
29 East 21st Street, New York, NY 10010

First Edition

Editor: Theresa Morlock
Book Design: Tanya Dellaccio

Photo Credits: Cover, back cover, pp. 1, 3–6, 8–14, 16–18, 20–24 Joost van Uffelen/Shutterstock.com; p. 5 (top) Irina No/Shutterstock.com; p, 5 (bottom) Croisy/Shutterstock.com; p. 6 Nonchanon/Shutterstock.com; p. 7 HOMONSTOCK/Shutterstock.com; p. 9 (top) Paul Vinten/Shutterstock.com; p. 9 (bottom) vkilikov/Shutterstock.com; pp. 11 (top), 16 Willyam Bradberry/Shutterstock.com; p. 11 (bottom) k_samurkas/Shutterstock.com; p. 12 Halyna Parinova/Shutterstock/com; p. 13 (top) Rene Frederick/Photodisc/Getty Images; pp. 13 (bottom), 15, 17 (top), 17 (bottom) Andrea Izzotti/Shutterstock.com; p. 18 Leonardo Gonzalez/Shutterstock.com; p. 19 Alexander Safonov/Moment Select/Getty Images; p. 21 (top) Jeff Rotman Photography/Corbis Documentary/Getty Images; p. 21 (bottom) MIGUEL ROJO/AFP/Getty Images.

Cataloging-in-Publication Data

Names: MacDhui, Lori.
Title: How do dolphins communicate? / Lori MacDhui.
Description: New York : PowerKids Press, 2018. | Series: How life science works | Includes index.
Identifiers: ISBN 9781508156451 (pbk.) | ISBN 9781508156390 (library bound) | ISBN 9781508156277 (6 pack)
Subjects: LCSH: Dolphins–Juvenile literature. | Animal communication–Juvenile literature.
Classification: LCC QL737.C432 M33 2018 | DDC 599.53-dc23

Manufactured in the United States of America

CPSIA Compliance Information: Batch #BS17PK For Further Information contact Rosen Publishing, New York, New York at 1-800-237-9932

CONTENTS

DELIGHTFUL DOLPHINS

There are few creatures as delightful as dolphins! Their curved mouths make them look as though they're always smiling. Their playful behaviors are fun to watch. Dolphins are commonly thought of as the smartest animals on Earth, with intelligence second only to humans. One of the most interesting things about dolphins is the way they communicate.

Dolphins use a range of noises to "talk" to each other. They communicate information to hunt as a team, to play together, and to help each other avoid predators. Scientists are just beginning to understand the mystery of dolphin communication.

SCIENTISTS DISAGREE ABOUT WHETHER OR NOT DOLPHIN NOISES CAN BE THOUGHT OF AS A LANGUAGE.

BOTTLENOSE BEAUTIES

There are more than 35 species, or kinds, of ocean dolphins. This book focuses on bottlenose dolphins, which are perhaps the most commonly known dolphins because they can often be seen in aquariums.

Bottlenose dolphins live in warm, **tropical** oceans. They're mammals and breathe air using a blowhole at the top of their head. Adult bottlenose dolphins are about 10 to 14 feet (3 to 4.3 m) long and can weigh up to 1,100 pounds (499 kg). They swim at speeds up to 18 miles (29 km) per hour.

Bottlenose dolphins can be trained to perform tricks and are able to understand human commands.

PLAYFUL PODS

Dolphins are highly social animals. They live in groups called pods, which can have around 20 members. Sometimes pods join together to form larger groups called herds.

Common types of dolphin groups include groups of females and their calves, or babies, groups of young males and females together, and groups of two adult males. Dolphins in a pod **cooperate** with each other to find food, protect their calves, and **defend** one another against attackers. Adult males may form partnerships called pair bonds to work together to win mates. Members of pods come and go as they form new bonds.

CALVES AND MOTHERS SHARE A CLOSE BOND. CALVES MAY STAY WITH THEIR MOTHERS FOR UP TO SIX YEARS. IN THE WILD, BOTTLENOSE DOLPHINS LIVE FOR 45 TO 50 YEARS.

FUNNY FRIENDS

Scientists have observed that dolphins form friendships. They show **affection** by resting their fins on their friends, similar to the way people hold hands. Dolphins play by chasing each other, throwing seaweed at each other, and breaching, or jumping out of the water.

Not all dolphin interactions are friendly ones. When they're upset, dolphins may bite, blow bubbles from their blowhole, clap their jaws together, or smack their tail on the water. They sometimes drag their teeth against another dolphin's skin when they are angry. This is called raking, and it doesn't seriously hurt the other dolphin.

Bottlenose dolphins can breach up to 20 feet (6 m) in the air!

CHEERFUL CHATTER

Dolphins speak to each other using **vocalizations** such as clicks, squeaks, and whistles. Dolphins use whistles to identify each other. Each dolphin has its own **unique** whistle that is just like a name. When a mother gives birth to a calf, she whistles to it for days so the calf will learn to recognize her particular whistle. Calves develop their own whistle by the time they're a month old.

Dolphins whistle for several reasons. If they're separated from their group, they may whistle to find each other. They also whistle to call for help. Sometimes dolphins **imitate** other dolphins' whistles.

Scientists have observed dolphins helping other dolphins in need. They've also been known to help whales and people.

NASAL NOISES

Unlike people, dolphins don't have **vocal cords**. Instead they make noises by pushing air through their nasal passages, or the channels through their nose. Inside a dolphin's nasal passages are two sets of structures called phonic lips. As air is pushed through these lips, it creates sounds. Dolphins can use their two sets of phonic lips at the same time, meaning they can both whistle and click at once.

Dolphins produce two types of vocalizations: pure sounds and pulsed sounds. Whistles and squeaks are pure sounds. Clicks are quick, short vocalizations and are considered pulsed sounds.

Sound travels through water 4.5 times faster than it travels through air. That's why dolphins rely on vocalizing to communicate.

EXTRAORDINARY ECHOLOCATION

Dolphins use clicks to learn about their surroundings. This special ability is called echolocation. To use echolocation, the dolphin clicks and listens as the sound is **reflected** off objects and creatures in the water nearby. The reflected sound wave, or echo, travels over the dolphin's lower jaw to its inner ear, sending a message to its brain.

Based on the reflected sound wave, the dolphin is able to identify the object and how far away it is. Dolphins use echolocation to avoid predators, find prey, and **navigate** through the ocean.

Dolphins can identify the shape, size, speed, and location of an object or creature in the water based on the way sound bounces off it!

ECHOLOCATION

SOUND WAVES MADE BY DOLPHIN

ECHOS OF SOUND

TRUSTY TEAMMATES

When dolphins locate their prey, they communicate with each other to hunt as a team. Bottlenose dolphins are carnivores, which means they only eat meat. Their diet is mostly made up of fish, shrimp, and squid.

Dolphins use several methods to catch prey. One method is to create a "bait ball." A group of dolphins will swim in a tight circle around a school of fish, working as a team to drive the fish closer together. When the fish are in a tight ball, unable to escape, the dolphins then take turns eating the fish.

BAIT BALL

DOLPHINS HAVE BEEN OBSERVED WORKING WITH FISHERMEN BY DRIVING THE FISH TOWARD THE FISHERMEN. THIS MAKES THE FISH EASIER TO CATCH. THE DOLPHINS THEN SHARE IN THE FISHY FEAST.

DOLPHIN DEFENSES

Dolphins rely on communication to avoid predators, such as sharks. They use echolocation to locate predators and squeak and whistle to warn their friends that danger is nearby. If attacked, dolphins work together to defend every member of the pod. They use their speed and strength to ram the predator, driving it away.

Dolphins are one of the ocean's top predators. For the most part, their cooperation protects them from attacks. Unfortunately, people are the greatest danger to dolphins. Pollution harms dolphins' ocean homes and they're often accidentally killed when caught in fishing nets.

THIS DOLPHIN CALF WAS RESCUED AFTER BEING CAUGHT IN A FISHING NET. FISHING COMPANIES THAT USE "DOLPHIN SAFE" LABELS ON THEIR PRODUCTS MAKE AN EFFORT TO AVOID HARMING DOLPHINS.

CLEVER CREATURES

Dolphins are very clever creatures. Scientists recently discovered that dolphins recognize themselves in mirrors. This is important because it shows they have self-awareness. Dolphins also use tools to accomplish tasks. They even play tricks on other animals, which could show they have a sense of humor.

Some scientists believe that dolphins talk to each other just like people do, having conversations about their feelings and daily events. People are just beginning to understand how dolphins think and communicate. As scientists continue to study dolphins, we may continue to be surprised by what they find.

GLOSSARY

affection: A feeling of fondness or love.

cooperate: To work together.

defend: To guard from harm.

imitate: To copy something or someone else.

navigate: To find one's way.

reflect: To throw back light, heat, or sound.

tropical: Having to do with warm parts of the Earth that are near the equator.

unique: Being the only one of its kind.

vocal cords: Two small bands of body tissue that move to make sounds when air moves over them.

vocalization: A noise or sound produced by a living creature.

INDEX

WEBSITES

Due to the changing nature of Internet links, PowerKids Press has developed an online list of websites related to the subject of this book. This site is updated regularly. Please use this link to access the list:
www.powerkidslinks.com/ls/dol